CO-EXIST KUWAIT:
QUOTES AND NOTES

Nejoud Al-Yagout

Note to the Reader:

Co-Exist Kuwait was founded in January 2017 as a result of a growing tolerance, and simultaneously, growing intolerance for those we erroneously consider minorities – locally and globally. Amazingly, according to mystics, the greater the light, the darker the shadow, so this is not worrisome. Not one bit. In fact, the response to the call for coexistence is an indication that fear is surrendering, finally, to love. All the quotes and notes in the following pages were written and compiled by the founder of Co-Exist Kuwait: Nejoud Al-Yagout.

The ocean does not deprive anyone of its bounties due to one's skin color, belief system or gender.

There are no red carpets or first class lounges in orchards and vineyards.

Deserts and forests know no borders or checkpoints.

The sky does not label anyone as an expatriate or minority.

Ain't nature grand?

The expatriate includes the mother who works tirelessly in our homes and whose passport is taken from her; the father who runs our errands and is terrified of having his license revoked; the son who sweeps the streets but does not always get paid; the uncle who left his family behind to dabble in investment banking yet living in fear that any day his job may be given to a local; the daughter who teaches our children but is too ashamed to discuss her faith publicly.

There are no expatriates when we coexist. We are all diverse souls on a journey, far from home. That's all.

When we are asleep to the reality of intolerance, no seeds of love can grow.

Does it not break our collective hearts that there are mosques in every corner, only a handful of churches and that's about it? The outer world can only be transformed when we heal from within, when we free our inner selves from the yokes of conditioning.

Here's to planting a tree of coexistence.

Here's to awakening.

And we have been taught that we are superior to the other.

And we have been taught to be suspicious of the other.

And we have been taught to convert the other to our way.

And we have been taught that the other is an infidel who must be destroyed.

And we have been taught that the Divine plays favorites.

And we have been taught never to befriend the other.

But we were not taught that we *are* the other.

The word "expat" is a dirty word. Anyone living inside the man-made borders of any given country is, in fact, a local.

The word minority is another dirty word. It is divisive and polarizes us – further fueling the ego while inviting delusions of grandeur.

There are no expats: only travelers in the vast expanse.

There are no minorities: only colors in the divine palette of consciousness.

Unconditional love is not just love without conditions, but a love free from conditioning as well.

It's considered brave to speak of love in a world of fear.

How tragic is that?

Love is our nature. It is not an act of courage.

And we can't afford to have it any other way.

The greatest downfall of humanity is not using our calling to raise the frequency on our planet.

This is not about protesting, having discussions, hosting debates, blaming or complaining. This is about each of us using our divine outlets to make a difference whether through music, art, poetry, writing, dancing, cooking, acting, raising children, teaching or directing. Our calling is a gift we were given to eradicate the parts of us that discriminate.

We will never be ready, so we might as well begin now.

We were not born to convene in structures that accept only those who are like us. We were born to recognize the unified temple of our hearts.

We were not born to appease the divine. We were born to celebrate Source.

We were not born to segregate based upon gender or race. We were born to dance with one another.

We were not born to classify each other as rich or poor. We were born to share the sufficient resources on our planet.

We were not born to judge each other. We were born to enjoy the multifaceted expressions of consciousness.

We were not born to ostracize each other. We were born to coexist.

Coexistence means that even though we were taught to convert you, or close down your temple, we instead choose to accept you and defend your right to worship.

Coexistence means that though we have residual fear, we choose to go against it in the name of love.

Coexistence means that we acknowledge that each society sees non-citizens as others, but we embrace foreigners as sisters and brothers.

Coexistence means that even when our egos call us hypocrites or tell us we are hiding our beliefs or prejudices, we know that any racism lurking within us was taught, and by observing the thoughts without acting upon them or judging ourselves, we are able to create a space for love to flourish even amidst any inner conflict.

Compassion is a prophet.

Universality, a religion.

Creativity – scripture.

Awakening: the afterlife.

We are the angels and demons.

The infidels: anger, jealousy, greed, hate, intolerance.

Kiss the sinners and saints.

Connect in the space where the godless and the godly are one.

Make love to nothingness and everything.

Embrace the path and no path.

Come empty and leave full.

We are not just brothers and sisters.

We are each other.

We don't have to like everyone to coexist, nor do we have to agree with others' ideologies, lifestyles, choices or inclinations.

Coexistence means we honor the right of each individual to be an individual regardless of how *we* feel about it. Because we can bet that the person who we are judging is not too fond of what we adhere to either. Only the ego gives a damn. So let's change the station when it interferes with the frequency.

Coexistence is not just about embracing diversity but about embracing uniqueness.

Nature ain't a sucker for clones.

In our community, we have Sikh-phobia, Buddhist-phobia, atheist-phobia, agnostic-phobia, Jain-phobia, Baha'i-phobia, Hindu-phobia, homophobia, gender-phobia, oh and transgender-phobia, infidel-phobia, Judeo-phobia, Christo-phobia, Druze-phobia, Zoroastrian-phobia, pagan-phobia, stateless-phobia, expat-phobia, sect-phobia and on and on ad infinitum. And yet, locally (and globally), the focus is on Islamophobia.

Something to ponder.

Can we cease debating who is on the "right" or "wrong" path? Can we stop trying to convert an "infidel" to a "believer" or try to make a "gay" person "straight"? Can the canvas, painted white by human beings, finally become a masterpiece portraying the glory of black and all colors of consciousness? Can the masculine merge with, rather than subjugate, the feminine energy? Can the rich and poor remember that paper, yes *paper*, can never define our essence? Can foreigners be treated as beloved guests rather than as minorities? Can all who live here be treated as locals? Can the stateless finally be honored for their loyalty and patience? Can our consciousness evolve to vibrate at a high frequency? We are one, manifested as diversity.

Let's coexist.

Who offended us?

Why are we holding on to antiquated prejudices?

Why do we fear coexistence?

Why do we hate the enemies of our forefathers?

How are we still stuck in the wars of days of yore?

The cycle is waiting for love to slice it open, so that it no longer revolves but, rather, evolves.

Our hate is in the way. Our pain is in the way.

But our hate and pain are also *the* way.

Let us look closely and see *who* is looking.

We got this.

Today, we have the freedom and the means to live where our hearts guide us to, essentially. Thus, we are close to realizing our connectedness to all sentient beings, and not just to human beings.

A new way of living in harmony with Earth, animals, fish and insects is our next rung on the ladder of ascension.

Coexistence is not about forgiveness or being a good or peaceful person. It grows from authenticity and an acknowledgment of our discomfort around certain people due to political, ideological and personal differences, but defending their rights, regardless.

It is no longer about tolerance or tolerating, but about remembrance and returning.

When we are asleep:

sex trafficking *child prostitution* racism *minorities* refugees *competitiveness* invasion *expansionism* patriarchy *divisiveness* labeling *discrimination* statelessness *class system* money *financial imbalance* war *abuse* harassment *rape* violence *hunger* poverty *slavery* genocide *proselytizing* censorship *sabotage* tactics *control* monopoly *indoctrination* conditioning *manipulation* terrorism *murder* dictatorship *honor killings* exploitation *mistreatment of animals and sentient beings* hatred *pollution* pesticides *dumping waste* unjust distribution of resources *hoarding* disregard for the environment *intimidation* ideology *greed* fear

When we are awake:

love

Human beings, regardless of their belief systems, cannot afford to allow fear to be a guide. The state of the world itself is a testament to the consequences of doing so. For those who adhere to religion, here lies an invitation for scholars and followers to quote religious tolerance inherent in scripture. And for those who do not, there is a calling to remember that tolerance is imprinted in our core.

The time is upon us, as we evolve in consciousness, to remind ourselves that silence keeps the status quo in place. We have a moral responsibility to express our dismay if we were born here, without blaming or protesting, to remind each other of our oneness.

Does it matter if you use beads or wear garlands?

Does it matter whether you dance to the tune of the crescent and star, the cross, the star of David, the *khanda*, countless deities or nothing at all – yes, nothing at all.

Does it matter if you are the yin to the yang or whether you bask in the realm of the rainbow? Does it matter if you see others as separate or believe in non-duality? Does it matter whether your skin is white or black, which tribe you come from; tell me: does it?

This is an invitation to let it all go. Our thoughts are killing each other. This is an invitation to love, to coexist.

Unity starts within us, individually, then expands to our community and then spreads its tentacles across the globe.

Befriend the other.

You *are* the other.

9 781987 617689